TABLETOP WARS
CASTLE ATTACK
Make Your Own Medieval Battlefield

Thanks to the creative team:
Senior Editor: Alice Peebles
Fact checking: Kate Mitchell
Design: www.collaborate.agency

Hungry Tomato™
A division of Lerner Publishing Group, Inc.
241 First Avenue North
Minneapolis, MN 55401 USA

For reading levels and more information, look up
this title at www.lernerbooks.com.

Main body text set in Bodoni 72.
Typeface provided by International Typeface Corp.

Library of Congress Cataloging-in-Publication Data
Names: Ives, Rob, author. | De Quay, John Paul, illustrator.
Title: Castle attack : make your own medieval battlefield / Rob Ives ;
  illustrated by John Paul de Quay.
Description: Minneapolis, MN : Hungry Tomato, [2017]. | Series:
  Tabletop wars | Audience: Ages 8-12. | Audience: Grades 4 to 6. |
  Includes index.
Identifiers: LCCN 2016012043 (print) | LCCN 2016014911
  (ebook) | ISBN 9781512406399 (lb : alk. paper) | ISBN
  9781512411713 (pb : alk. paper) | ISBN 9781512409260
  (eb pdf)
Subjects: LCSH: Castles—Design and construction—Juvenile
  literature. | Sieges—Juvenile literature. | Models and
  modelmaking—Juvenile literature.
Classification: LCC UG444 .I94 2017 (print) | LCC UG444
  (ebook) | DDC 728.8/1—dc23

LC record available at http://lccn.loc.gov/2016012043

Manufactured in the United States of America
1-39312-21149-4/28/2016

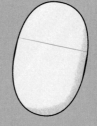

TABLETOP WARS
CASTLE ATTACK
Make Your Own Medieval Battlefield

by Rob Ives

Illustrated by John Paul de Quay

HUNGRY TOMATO™

Minneapolis

Safety First!

Take care and use good sense when making your own medieval battlefield. Even though the models are small, and you may use soft missiles with the weapons made in other books in this series, the unexpected can happen. Be responsible and always be safe.

Bolts, darts, and other missiles can cause damage when fired with force. Never point the launchers or aim anything at people, animals, or anything of value.

Look for the safety warning sign in the activities and ask an adult for assistance when you are cutting materials.

Watch for this sign throughout the book. You may need help from an adult to complete these tasks.

CONTENTS

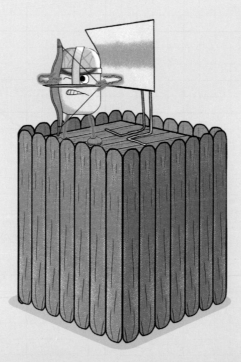

MEDIEVAL CASTLE

This book shows you how to make small, fun models of the key structures of a castle, a trusty fighting force to defend it, and a siege tower to attack it. Line up your knights on the battlements and await the fiendish enemy!

Supply List:

To make the amazing fortifications, knights, and siege tower in this book, you will need these supplies. Most items can be found at home, school, or a craft store.

Corrugated Cardboard

Thick Card

Plastic Easter Eggs

Cardboard Tube

Heavy Thread

Felt-tip Pens

Long Paper Clips

Coffee Stirrers

Wooden Craft Sticks

Pencils

Pen (for marking)

Rubber Bands

Googly Eyes

Aluminum Foil

Large Wooden Skewers 12 inches (30.5 cm) long

Pipe Cleaners

Small Wooden Skewers 4 inches (10 cm) long

Marker Pen

Building Castles

Medieval stone castles were built all over Europe and the Middle East from about 1000–1500 CE. They were so invincible that many can be seen today, still in very good shape. Now you can make their key elements—towers, drawbridge, and portcullis—in miniature form.

If your battlements fall, though, they'll be easy to replace! Human defenders are also hugely important in sieges, of course, so make an army of knights! Then see how you can storm all these defenses with a soaring siege tower.

All you need are some easy-to-find supplies. Then follow the step-by-step instructions and in no time you'll be in charge of a super-strong castle!

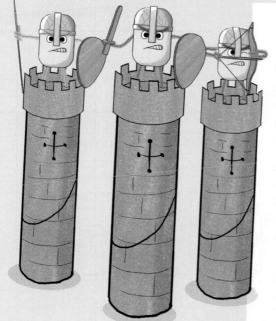

TIPS

Some projects ask for pencils to be cut into sections. Ask for help with this and use a cutting mat to cut on. An efficient way to do this is to cut each face of the pencil, and then snap it apart. Tidy up any unevenness with a craft knife.

Also ask for help when cutting the barrel of a pen—this can be quite tricky! One way of doing it neatly is to use a file to make a notch all the way around the barrel and then snap off the piece.

Use the sharp point of a pencil to make small holes in cardboard. Or ask an adult to help with this, using scissors or a craft knife.

Tools Needed:

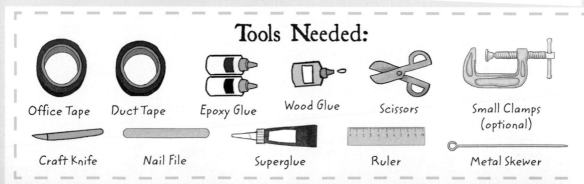

Office Tape   Duct Tape   Epoxy Glue   Wood Glue   Scissors   Small Clamps (optional)

Craft Knife   Nail File   Superglue   Ruler   Metal Skewer

KNIGHTS

Fortified castles are no good without a trusty standing army! You too must have a fearsome, well-armed force skilled with the bow, sword, and battle-ax, ready to protect your castle at all times.

Supplies:

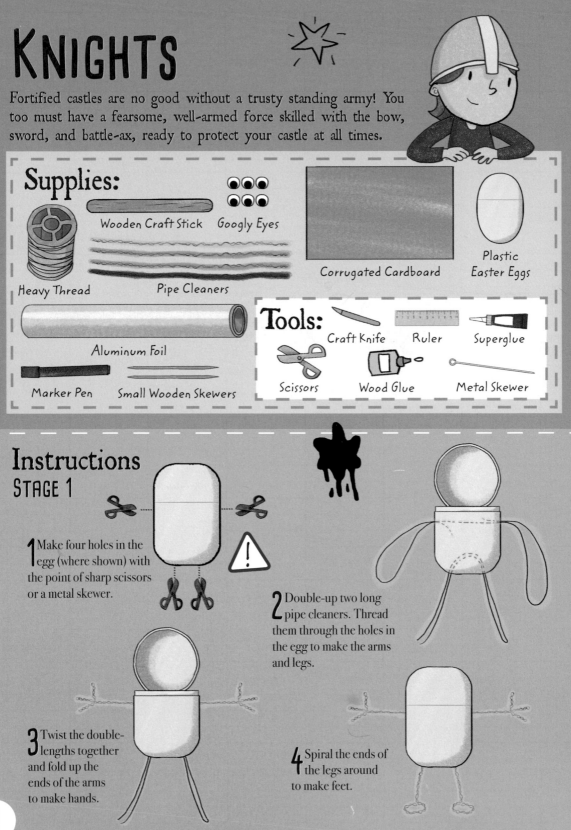

Wooden Craft Stick   Googly Eyes

Heavy Thread   Pipe Cleaners

Corrugated Cardboard

Plastic Easter Eggs

Aluminum Foil

Marker Pen   Small Wooden Skewers

Tools:

Craft Knife   Ruler   Superglue

Scissors   Wood Glue   Metal Skewer

Instructions
STAGE 1

1 Make four holes in the egg (where shown) with the point of sharp scissors or a metal skewer.

2 Double-up two long pipe cleaners. Thread them through the holes in the egg to make the arms and legs.

3 Twist the double-lengths together and fold up the ends of the arms to make hands.

4 Spiral the ends of the legs around to make feet.

8

5 Cut out a small piece of foil to fit around the egg. Fold the edge several times to make a rim for the helmet.

6 Fit the helmet around the egg, trimming off any excess. Glue it in place with superglue. Take care!

7 Fold over the end and smooth it down to make the top of the helmet.

8 Form a strip of foil eight to ten layers thick, measuring 0.2 x 3 inches (5 x 80 mm).

9 Use superglue to fix the strip into position with part overhanging as the nosepiece.

10 Cut a short length of pipe cleaner and glue it to the rim and under the nosepiece as eyebrows.

11 Glue on two googly eyes.

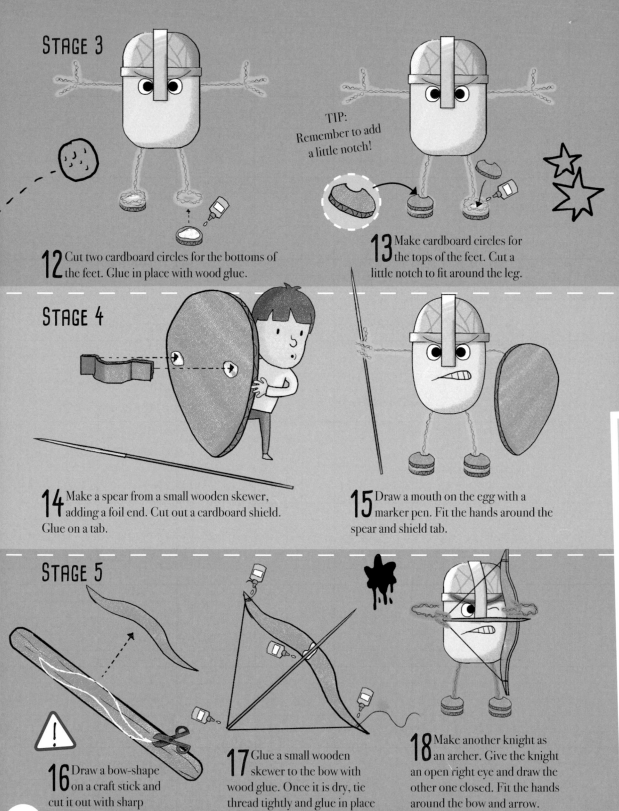

STAGE 3

12 Cut two cardboard circles for the bottoms of the feet. Glue in place with wood glue.

TIP:
Remember to add
a little notch!

13 Make cardboard circles for the tops of the feet. Cut a little notch to fit around the leg.

STAGE 4

14 Make a spear from a small wooden skewer, adding a foil end. Cut out a cardboard shield. Glue on a tab.

15 Draw a mouth on the egg with a marker pen. Fit the hands around the spear and shield tab.

STAGE 5

16 Draw a bow-shape on a craft stick and cut it out with sharp scissors.

17 Glue a small wooden skewer to the bow with wood glue. Once it is dry, tie thread tightly and glue in place to make the bowstring.

18 Make another knight as an archer. Give the knight an open right eye and draw the other one closed. Fit the hands around the bow and arrow.

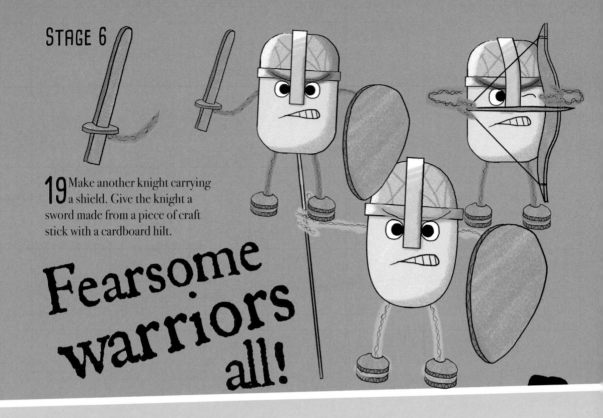

STAGE 6

19 Make another knight carrying a shield. Give the knight a sword made from a piece of craft stick with a cardboard hilt.

Fearsome warriors all!

MEDIEVAL KNIGHTS

Up until approximately 1200, knights wore chain mail for protection, with a nasal helmet over a mail coif, or hood, to protect the head. Knights needed all this—and shields—to survive hand-to-hand fighting on the battlefield.

ROUND TOWER

Build a tall, round tower and post sentries to keep a sharp lookout. Sound the alarm when the enemy appears, and get ready to rain down arrows. Your tower's so tough, it won't collapse!

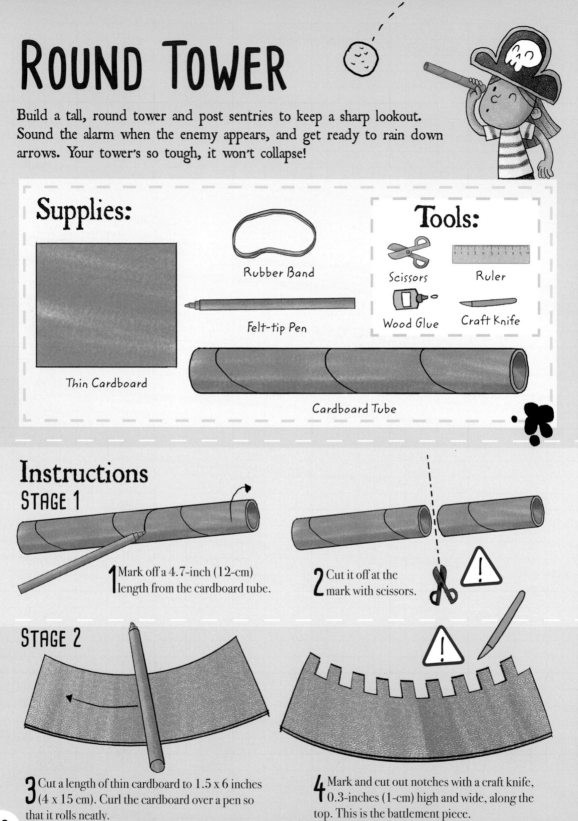

Supplies:

Rubber Band

Felt-tip Pen

Thin Cardboard

Cardboard Tube

Tools:

Scissors

Ruler

Wood Glue

Craft Knife

Instructions

STAGE 1

1 Mark off a 4.7-inch (12-cm) length from the cardboard tube.

2 Cut it off at the mark with scissors.

STAGE 2

3 Cut a length of thin cardboard to 1.5 x 6 inches (4 x 15 cm). Curl the cardboard over a pen so that it rolls neatly.

4 Mark and cut out notches with a craft knife, 0.3-inches (1-cm) high and wide, along the top. This is the battlement piece.

STAGE 3

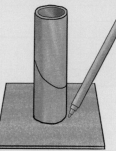

5 Draw around the end of the tube on a piece of cardboard.

6 Cut out the circle.

7 Roll the battlement piece around the top of the tube. Make sure it is the correct length and then glue it in place with wood glue. Wrap a rubber band around it to hold it in place until the glue dries. Fit the cardboard circle on top of the tube.

8 Draw bricks and windows on the tower with a felt-tip pen. Add a soldier . . .

or three!

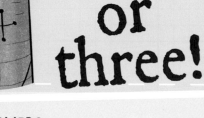

ROUND TOWERS

Unlike a square tower, a round tower had no weak points. It had no corners that the enemy could dig below to make the tower collapse. The circular design was first developed in France in approximately 1125. The enemy had to concentrate on pummeling the walls, while archers on the battlements fired arrows from the open gaps.

DRAWBRIDGE

Imagine your enemy got across your stagnant, smelly moat. (They don't care about the stink as they haven't had a bath for weeks anyway.) Pull up the drawbridge double-quick—they mustn't get their hands on your candy stash.

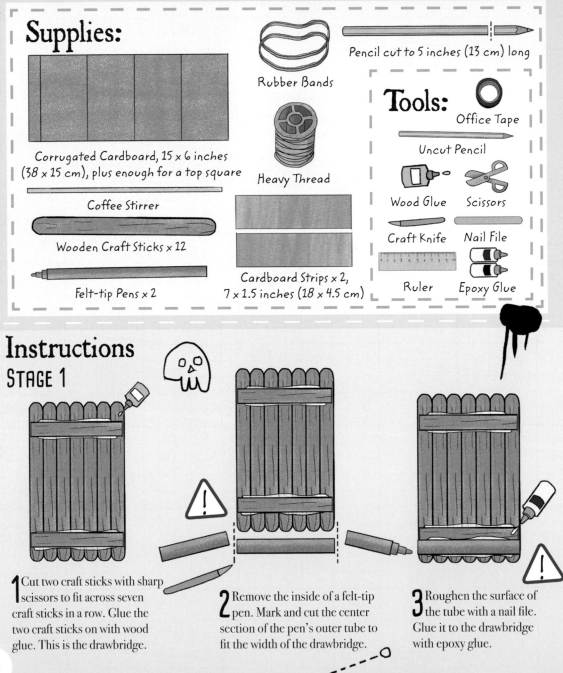

Supplies:

Corrugated Cardboard, 15 x 6 inches (38 x 15 cm), plus enough for a top square

Coffee Stirrer

Wooden Craft Sticks x 12

Felt-tip Pens x 2

Rubber Bands

Pencil cut to 5 inches (13 cm) long

Heavy Thread

Cardboard Strips x 2, 7 x 1.5 inches (18 x 4.5 cm)

Tools:

Office Tape

Uncut Pencil

Wood Glue   Scissors

Craft Knife   Nail File

Ruler   Epoxy Glue

Instructions
STAGE 1

1 Cut two craft sticks with sharp scissors to fit across seven craft sticks in a row. Glue the two craft sticks on with wood glue. This is the drawbridge.

2 Remove the inside of a felt-tip pen. Mark and cut the center section of the pen's outer tube to fit the width of the drawbridge.

3 Roughen the surface of the tube with a nail file. Glue it to the drawbridge with epoxy glue.

STAGE 2

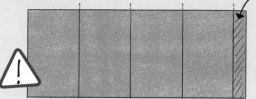

Margin

4 Cut a 15 x 6-inch (38 x 15-cm) piece of cardboard with the flutes running vertically. Score four vertical lines (do not cut all the way through), using a ruler and craft knife, that are 3.5-inches (9-cm) apart.

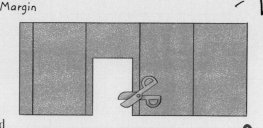

5 Mark and cut out a door hole that is 0.2 inches (0.5 cm) wider than the drawbridge, but not as tall.

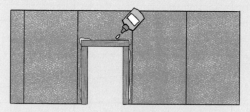

6 Frame the door with craft sticks cut to length and glue them in place with wood glue.

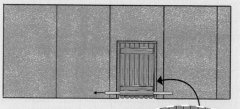

7 Flip the cardboard over to the back. Thread a coffee stirrer through the pen tube.

STAGE 3

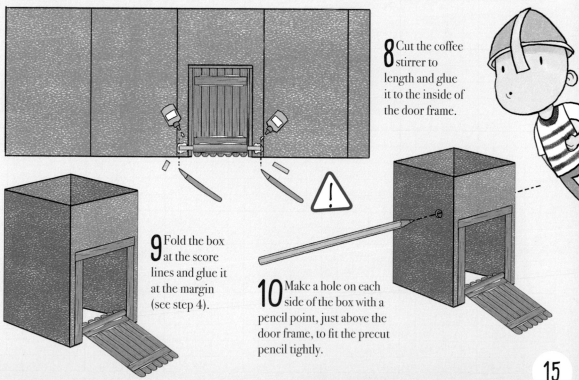

8 Cut the coffee stirrer to length and glue it to the inside of the door frame.

9 Fold the box at the score lines and glue it at the margin (see step 4).

10 Make a hole on each side of the box with a pencil point, just above the door frame, to fit the precut pencil tightly.

15

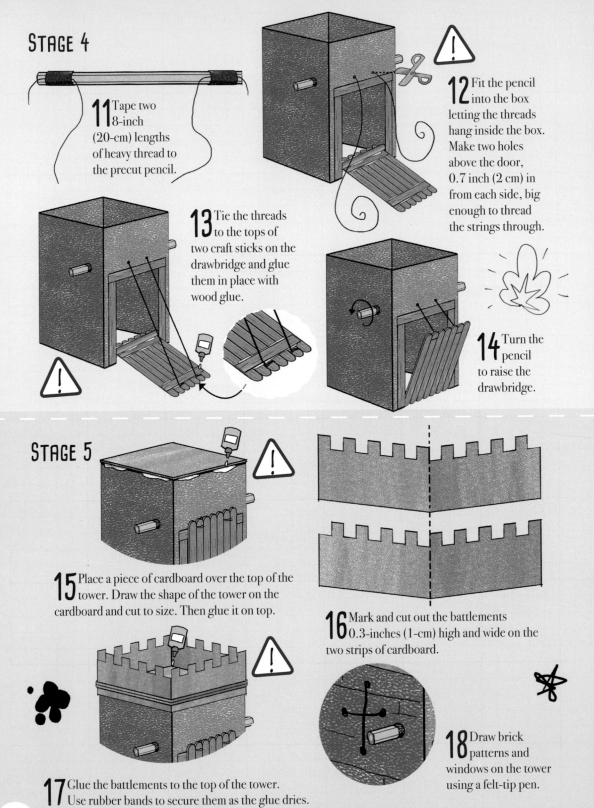

STAGE 4

11 Tape two 8-inch (20-cm) lengths of heavy thread to the precut pencil.

12 Fit the pencil into the box letting the threads hang inside the box. Make two holes above the door, 0.7 inch (2 cm) in from each side, big enough to thread the strings through.

13 Tie the threads to the tops of two craft sticks on the drawbridge and glue them in place with wood glue.

14 Turn the pencil to raise the drawbridge.

STAGE 5

15 Place a piece of cardboard over the top of the tower. Draw the shape of the tower on the cardboard and cut to size. Then glue it on top.

16 Mark and cut out the battlements 0.3-inches (1-cm) high and wide on the two strips of cardboard.

17 Glue the battlements to the top of the tower. Use rubber bands to secure them as the glue dries.

18 Draw brick patterns and windows on the tower using a felt-tip pen.

19 Place a guard on the roof and . . .

Lower the drawbridge!

MEDIEVAL DRAWBRIDGE

In many castles, just a wooden plank over the moat served as the drawbridge. It opened out from the gatehouse—the fortified main entrance. The enemy would be bombarded with missiles to keep them off the drawbridge. Then the drawbridge was pulled up on chains or by a system of weights. The drawbridge formed an extra barrier and, hopefully, kept the enemy on the outside!

Portcullis

This trusty defensive gate was invented by the Romans but really stood the test of time. Your cunning enemy is over the drawbridge and at the castle entrance . . . now snap the portcullis into place!

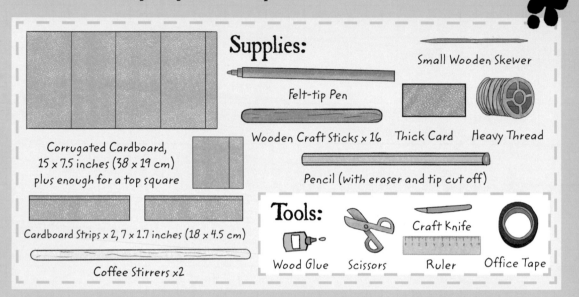

Supplies:

Felt-tip Pen

Small Wooden Skewer

Wooden Craft Sticks x 16

Thick Card

Heavy Thread

Corrugated Cardboard, 15 x 7.5 inches (38 x 19 cm) plus enough for a top square

Pencil (with eraser and tip cut off)

Cardboard Strips x 2, 7 x 1.7 inches (18 x 4.5 cm)

Coffee Stirrers x2

Tools:

Wood Glue

Scissors

Craft Knife

Ruler

Office Tape

Instructions
STAGE 1

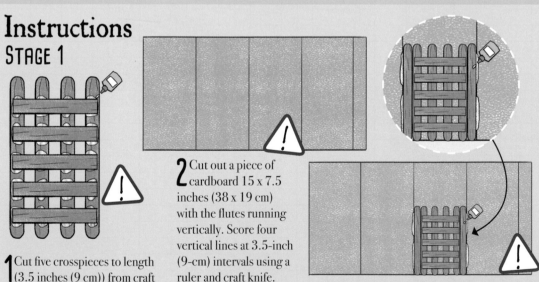

1 Cut five crosspieces to length (3.5 inches (9 cm)) from craft sticks with sharp scissors. Glue them to four craft sticks and let them dry under a heavy book.

2 Cut out a piece of cardboard 15 x 7.5 inches (38 x 19 cm) with the flutes running vertically. Score four vertical lines at 3.5-inch (9-cm) intervals using a ruler and craft knife.

3 Place the portcullis inside the back of one of the cardboard sections. Lay a craft stick on each side and glue down with wood glue. Don't glue the portcullis down!

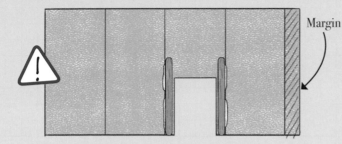

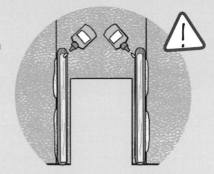

Margin

4 Cut out a doorway 0.2 inch (3 mm) from the sides of the craft sticks and 1 inch (25 mm) below the top of the craft sticks.

5 Cut two coffee stirrers the same length as the craft sticks. Glue one to the inside edge of each craft stick.

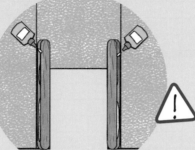

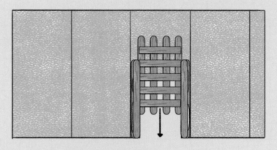

6 Glue on a second craft stick (on both sides) so that its outer edge lines up with the coffee stirrer's edge.

7 When the glue is completely dry, slide the portcullis into place.

8 On the other side of the cardboard, frame the door with two craft sticks at the sides cut to length. Add one at the top cut to the overall width.

9 Fold the box at the scored lines and glue along the margin (see step 4).

19

STAGE 2

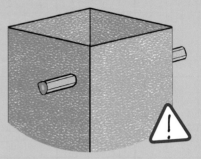

10 Tape a 8-inch (20-cm) length of heavy thread to the center of the precut pencil.

11 Make two holes in the box 0.5 inch (15 mm) from the front and 1 inch (25 mm) down with a pencil or scissors. The holes should be a tight fit for the pencil. Fit the precut pencil into the box.

12 Tie the thread's other end to the center of the portcullis after the pencil is in the box (shown here outside the box so you can see where to tie the thread).

STAGE 3

13 Mark and cut notches 0.3-inches (1-cm) high and wide on the two cardboard strips.

14 Cut a square of cardboard to fit the top of the tower. Glue it on with wood glue. Glue the battlement strips into place.

15 Add a flag made from a small skewer and colored card. Draw windows and bricks on the tower with a felt-tip pen.

STAGE 4

16 Turn the pencil to raise the portcullis!

17 Set a guard to . . .

Protect your castle!

ANCIENT PORTCULLIS

The Romans designed this heavy, grilled gate to defend their cities. It dropped vertically into place to halt an enemy's attack, penning them in while they were bombarded from above. In a medieval castle, the portcullis trapped the enemy at the entrance, exposing enemies to arrows and boiling oil dropped from above.

SIEGE TOWER

Now it's your turn to make an assault on a castle with a mighty siege tower. The ancient Greeks handed down the technology and it was effective for thousands of years—a great way to defend your army when you're on the attack.

Supplies:

Corrugated Cardboard

Wooden Craft Sticks (roughly 50)

Large Wooden Skewers

Felt-tip Pens x 2

Coffee Stirrers x 3

Tools:

Ruler

Scissors   Craft Knife

Epoxy Glue   Wood Glue

Small Clamps (optional)

Instructions
STAGE 1

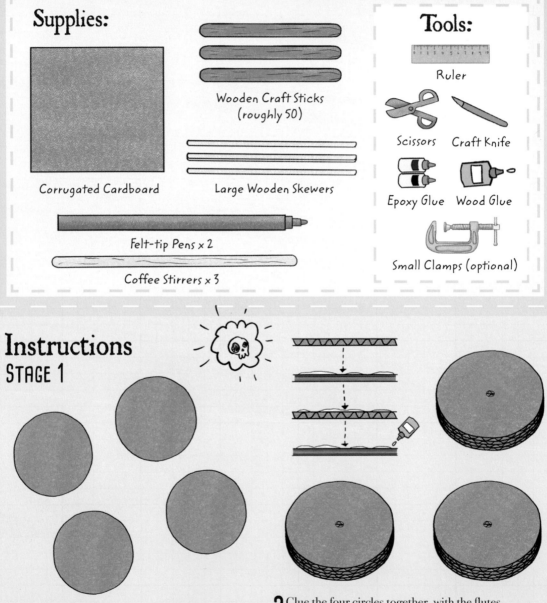

1 The wheels are made from cardboard. Cut four identical circles 1.2 inches (30 mm) in diameter to make one wheel.

2 Glue the four circles together, with the flutes facing different directions for maximum strength. Make three more wheels in the same way. Then push a wooden skewer though the center of each wheel.

STAGE 2

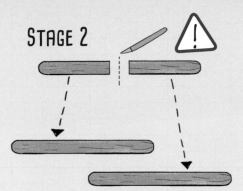

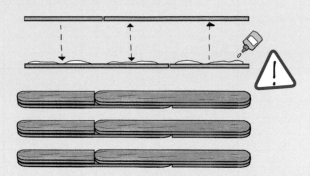

3 Cut a craft stick in half. Pair the halves with two other craft sticks.

4 Glue them together as above. Make three more the same—these will be the upright pieces of the tower.

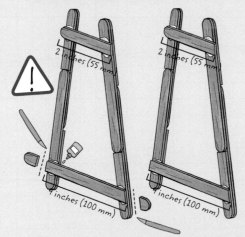

2 inches (55 mm)

4 inches (100 mm)

5 Glue craft stick crosspieces 0.5 inch (1.5 cm) from the top and bottom to the upright pieces. Trim the ends.

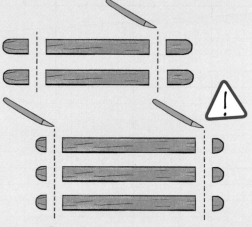

6 Cut craft sticks to 2.75 inches (70 mm) to make five crosspieces.

7 Add a third crosspiece to each side. Join the sides at the back with two crosspieces and at the front with one crosspiece at the bottom. Small clamps can help secure the crosspieces while the glue dries.

Stage 3

8 Work your way up the front gluing craft sticks in place as planking.

9 Cut craft sticks to length and add as diagonals to the sides.

10 Cut a platform to size from cardboard for the top. Glue it in place.

Stage 4

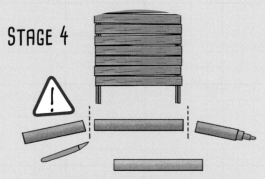

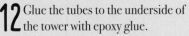

11 Cut two wheel axles from the outer tubes of felt-tip pens. They should be just slightly longer than the width of the tower.

12 Glue the tubes to the underside of the tower with epoxy glue.

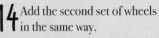

13 Use wooden skewers cut to length (the length of the axle tube, plus the width of two wheels, plus 1/8 inch (3 mm)). Thread one through an axle tube and glue the wheels into place at each end.

14 Add the second set of wheels in the same way.

STAGE 5

16 Glue the ladder to the back of the tower.

15 Make a ladder from two coffee stirrers. Cut the third coffee stirrer into 1.2-inch (30-mm) rungs and glue to make the ladder.

Invade!

MEDIEVAL SIEGE TOWER

A massive siege tower was built as tall as the castle under attack. Invaders wheeled the tower up against the castle walls and prepared for their attack. Inside the tower were several platforms that supported heavy siege weapons, such as catapults. Troops reached the higher levels by a ladder, and poured over battlements that had crumbled under bombardment.

CASTLE TOWER

Show no fear as you perch on top of your square tower watching for the enemy—you know they're out there. The tower might crumble under a fierce attack, but unlike a real one, it can be easily put back together!

Supplies:

Corrugated Cardboard, approximately 6 x 6 inches (15 x 15 cm)

Wooden Craft Sticks (roughly 60)

Long Paper Clip

Thick Card

Tools:

Scissors

Duct Tape

Wood Glue

Epoxy Glue

Instructions
STAGE 1

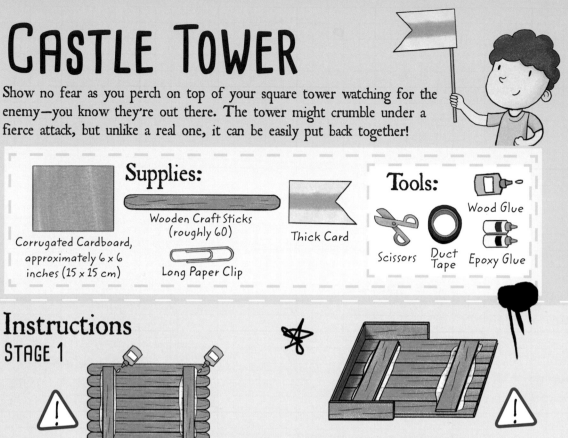

1 The four sides are each made from seven craft sticks and two crosspieces cut to length. Glue the craft sticks that form the sides. Position the crosspieces equally and glue them on.

2 Make the top of the tower from six craft sticks with the ends cut off. Glue together and add crosspieces cut to width. The lid is the same width, with 1.2-inch (30-mm) sides.

STAGE 2

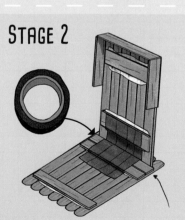

3 Fit a second crosspiece into position above the first one on one of the side pieces (arrowed) Tape the lid to the side so that it is free to move up and down.

4 Make a square base from two layers of cardboard. Cut them to the width of the tower walls and then glue them together. Arrange the sides around the base as shown.

5 Tape the sides to the base with strips of duct tape to make flexible joints.

STAGE 3

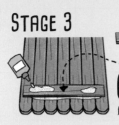 

6 On the side opposite the lid add a second crosspiece to make a double thickness on all four sides. Cut off the ends from a craft stick.

7 Glue two 0.5-inch (15-mm) lugs (craft stick pieces) to the crosspiece.

8 On the other two sides, add a single 0.5-inch (15-mm) lug to each crosspiece.

STAGE 4

9 Make a flagpole from a long paper clip. Glue the flagpole to the hinge end of the lid using epoxy glue. Make a 2.3 x 1.7-inch (6 x 4.5-cm) flag from thick card. Glue it to the flagpole. It needs to be stiff so when it is hit, the force lifts the lid.

10 Fold in the sides of the tower and catch them in place on the lugs.

A missile from a catapult or trebuchet may collapse the tower with a direct hit.

Defend!

MEDIEVAL TOWERS

Towers were the highest points of a castle structure. There were always several, positioned to give sweeping views in all directions in case of attack. Their thick walls had slits for firing arrows. Their height gave defenders a great opportunity to lob missiles down on the enemy.

THE FINISHED MODELS

These amazing models show just how impressive military machines and structures were in ancient and medieval times. Siege towers were used to bring down walls, but sturdy towers provided defense.

Knight

Active: From about the eighth to fifteenth centuries

Famous Examples: Knights Hospitaller and Knights Templar, twelfth century

Castle Tower

Square Towers Built By: European kings and military leaders, from the eleventh century

Famous Example: Rochester Castle, United Kingdom

Drawbridge

Built By: Medieval kings and military leaders

Famous Example: Muiderslot, moated castle, Netherlands

Portcullis

Built By: The Romans and medieval kings and leaders

Famous Example: Citadel of Carcassonne, France, from the third century

Round Tower

Built By: Medieval kings and knights

Famous Example: Krak des Chevaliers, Syria, eleventh to thirteenth centuries

Siege Tower

Built By: The Romans and Middle Eastern and European military leaders

Famous Example: Nine-story Helepolis (Taker of Cities), built by Demetrius I of Macedonia in 305 CE

CASTLE DEFENSE AND ATTACK

As castles became more strongly fortified with walls, portcullises, and skilled soldiers, attacking engines also became more fearsome.

Siege Tower

This powerful attacking engine was probably invented in ancient China, and was adopted by the Greeks and Romans. As it could only be effective when up against castle walls, the moat or ditch around a castle had to be filled up with rubble or dirt so the tower could be pushed into place. The tower was built on site to match the height of the walls under attack. Those within a castle might build a siege tower to oppose the attacking tower.

Barbican

If soldiers attacking a castle got over the moat and drawbridge, they reached the gatehouse (the heavily fortified entrance). Here soldiers entered a dangerous, narrow passageway called a barbican. As they streamed through, they might be trapped between two portcullises at either end. They could be fired on through narrow slits in the walls, or have boiling oil poured on them from holes overhead.

Knights

Trained from boyhood, knights became full-fledged warriors at sixteen to twenty years old. They served a lord, acting as his bodyguard, castle guard, and fighting force whenever wars broke out (which was often in medieval times). Knights took part in tournaments to practice swordsmanship and fighting skills on horseback. Even though they were not real battles, the knights could be injured or even killed at these tournaments.

Castle Walls

The outer wall that wrapped all around a castle was called a curtain wall. It had an inner core of rubble and was covered in huge stone blocks. This made the curtain wall very strong and able to withstand heavy weapons, such as battering rams. In about the mid-twelfth century, concentric castles were built, with at least one inner curtain wall inside the outer one. This made castles almost impossible to be breached and captured by invading forces. The area between the two walls was called the "death arena," because attackers encountered a rain of fire from the arrows of castle archers.

INDEX

THE AUTHOR

Rob Ives is a United Kingdom-based designer and paper engineer. He began making cardboard models as a math and science teacher, and then was asked to create two books of models. His published titles include *Paper Models that Rock!* and *Paper Automata*. He specializes in paper animations and projects, and often visits schools to talk about design technology and demonstrate his models.

THE ARTIST

John Paul de Quay is an illustrator with a BSc in Biology from the University of Sussex, United Kingdom, and has a postgraduate certificate in animation from the University of the West of England. He devotes his spare time to growing chili peppers, perfecting his plan for a sustainable future, and caring for a small plastic dinosaur. He has three pet squid that live in the bath, which makes drawing in ink quite economical . . .